STRENGTH FROM NATURE

STRENGTH FROM NATURE

SIMPLE LESSONS OF LIFE TAUGHT BY THE MOST
UNLIKELY MASTERS: THE NATURE TEACHERS

Cara Wilson-Granat

© 2017 Cara Wilson-Granat
All rights reserved.

ISBN: 197959788X
ISBN 13: 9781979597883
Library of Congress Control Number: 2017917557
CreateSpace Independent Publishing Platform
North Charleston, South Carolina

Human use, population, and technology have reached that certain stage where mother Earth no longer accepts our presence with silence.

—The Fourteenth Dalai Lama

Even if the end of the world would be imminent, you still must plant a tree today.

—Otto Frank, father of Anne Frank

In every walk with nature one receives far more than he seeks.

—JOHN MUIR

Until he extends his circle of compassion
to include all living things,
man will not himself find peace.

—ALBERT SCHWEITZER

When we show our respect for other living things,
they respond with respect for us.

-ARAPAHO

To Mother Nature and all the champion voices for all species dedicated to loving and protecting her— in particular, nature-lovers, activists, biologists, healers, teachers, students, spiritual leaders, eco-conscious lawyers, medical practitioners, animal rescuers, authors, journalists, poets, researchers, warriors, wildlife rangers, antipoachers, antivivisectionists, global warming leaders, photographers, artists, guides, writers, filmmakers, actors, gardeners, musicians, scientists, vegans, visionaries, and, most of all, my beloved children and grandchildren and all the children of the world—our planet's "trees of hope," and to beautiful Laura, my nature-loving sister, and Peter, my Rock. Thank you.

CONTENTS

Acknowledgments · xv
Introduction · xix

Chapter 1   The Stone and the Ripple Effect · · · · · · · · · · · · · · ·1
Chapter 2   The Pearl ·5
Chapter 3   The Rock and the Waves · · · · · · · · · · · · · · · · · ·8
Chapter 4   The Otter · 13
Chapter 5   The Spider · 17
Chapter 6   The River · 21
Chapter 7   The Aspen · 27
Chapter 8   The Butterfly · 31
Chapter 9   The Weed · 35
Chapter 10   The Yam · 38
Chapter 11   The Palm Tree · 41
Chapter 12   The Flower Pod and the Worm · · · · · · · · · · · · · 44
Chapter 13   The Cats · 46
Chapter 14   The Bird · 48
Chapter 15   Blind Birding by the Bay · · · · · · · · · · · · · · · · · 50
Chapter 16   The Nautilus · 55
Chapter 17   The Lobster · 59

Mother Nature Is Calling You · · · · · · · · · · · · · · · · · 63
Epilogue · 67
About the Author · 73
About the Illustrator · 75

When we tug at a single thing in nature,
we find it attached to the rest of the world.

—JOHN MUIR

The world is not comprehensible, but it is embraceable:
through the embracing of one of its beings.

—MARTIN BUBER

But ask the animals, and they will teach you;
the birds of the air, and they will tell you;
ask the plants of the earth, and they will teach you;
and the fish of the sea will declare to you.
Who among all these does not know
that the hand of the Lord has done this?
In his hand is the life of every living thing
and the breath of every human being.

JOB 12:7–10

I believe in God, only I spell it Nature.

—FRANK LLOYD WRIGHT

ACKNOWLEDGMENTS

SPECIAL THANKS TO my dear parents, Aaron and Lilly Weiss now heavenly guardian angels, who raised me and my sister, Laura, to love and embrace everything in the natural realm. Never were we stopped from cradling and taking home everything: broken ducks, lizards, all kinds of bugs, a tortoise, rabbits, dogs, birds, cats, chickens, roosters, goats, and even a hapless monkey. We learned to cherish them all.

We were such an odd bunch, my family. Dad was an executive director of a synagogue, and we lived on a small ranch nearby raising farm animals. Mother sold eggs out of her car on the weekends, and my parents had an incubator in their living room. My precious Hungarian grandma would can the fruit from an abundance of fruit trees on our property, and she even got bucked big time by our billy goat, evoking peals of laughter! How in the world these Jewish, Cleveland, Ohio, transplants ended up on a one-and-a-half-acre ranch for the purposes of milking goats and raising chickens and rabbits in Southern California's San Fernando Valley, I'll never know. But I loved that life and considered all of those little critters my extended family, as was profoundly evident when I screamed bloody epithets at my father after he decided to turn chicken farmer and attempt to kill and sell them for profit. (I say "attempt" because the bad stuff never happened.) I was so distraught, and my screams at him as I clung to the chicken coop weren't worth the emotional havoc it caused. Besides, he loved them too. Soon they all became pets, and in time the ranch was sold, much to my sister's and my dismay.

Nature was the hero—winning my heart and attention above all else. I loved nature more intensely than any religion. The world of flora and fauna was and continues to be where I gather spiritual sustenance. In my darkest hours, it is only Mother Nature that soothes me back to life. So it was only *natural* that this book became an homage to Nature Teachers.

I thank not only my dearest parents, but my beloved grandma Gizella, who never laughed at my passion for creatures large and small. One of my first memories of her was when I was a little child (in Cleveland) and had just learned a joyful song in kindergarten about a squirrel. Skipping down the street to my home, I suddenly saw a squashed squirrel quite dead in the street, and, hysterically sobbing (of course I thought it was the squirrel in the song!), I ran screaming to my grandma, who immediately held me, swept the little mammal into a shoebox, and helped me perform a funeral in our backyard surrounded by young neighborhood mourners. I'll never forget her compassion.

Another angel on Earth and now also in heaven was Benetta Fenimore, who shared my love for all things in nature—her kitchen was filled with fresh cuttings from every known plant; aquariums full of rescued bugs, spiders, and birds; vases of flowers; and on and on. When she visited me in Monterey, we would sit and watch the seals and gulls and wild ocean waves and share such healing beauty. Her spirit is everywhere within this book.

Special thanks go to Renée Owens, Patrick Hord, Steve Christianson, and Jane Cartmill, who offered their wisdom, compassion and vision to make sure I correctly covered some of the most important calls-to-action at the back of this book. To my dearest Marian Houser for her loving encouragement and wise counsel. To splendid Emily Tait for gracing this book with her beautiful illustrations and heart. And to Dr. Jane Goodall and Sy Montgomery, for inspiring hope and understanding and compassion in the world, one brilliant wildlife adventure/book/talk/action/documentary at a time.

Thanks also to the incredible family of friends at the Blind Community Center of San Diego, who awakened an *insight* I could have never imagined; you made my life so much richer. Special thanks to my birding buddy, Claude Edwards, who helped me appreciate the world of nature with a whole new sense of awareness, as he continues to do today.

And I thank the legions of angels here and above who've cheered me on each step of the way. There are far too many to mention. If I start listing names, someone's going to be pissed off or hurt because his or her name wasn't mentioned, so just know that I love you a lot and am grateful you're there. Thanks especially to my sons, Ethan Wilson and Jesse Wilson, who've always encouraged my dreams and shared their childhood with a passel of pets--as did Kent Wilson--we all adored, and to my stepson, Adam Granat, who showed up on my path with his Brittany doggy, Krissy, and his darling papa. To the next generation, I pass along this passion for life to my cherished Kaio and Nicholas and Autumn and Bly and Neiva and Katie and Dylan, and the myriad nieces and nephews, stepchildren, and inherited grandchildren who are tucked into my heart forevermore as well. And to all the wonderful dogs, cats, turtles and elephants past and present who have gifted my life with their purity and innocent acceptance—Terry, Ginger, Buffy, Gypsy, Huck, Zsa-Zsa, Madison, Lucky, Quince, Krissy, Jet, Rocky, Scout, Boo, Akeda, Tucker, Lukas, Greta, Pax, Pip, Daffy, Jag, Fig, Mogley, Pan, Suka, Blueberry, Shellby, Gita, Becky, Billy, Ruby, Sukari, and many, many guinea pigs (sweet Chunk), lizards, snakes, fish, birds, bunnies, and bugs as well. Finally, special thanks to my dearest Pete, who is the steady rock in my life and helped me at last come home to what is real and enduring, sharing the world of nature we both love so much. Blessings to all.

In all things in nature there is something of the marvelous.

—ARISTOTLE

INTRODUCTION

DAME JANE GOODALL (famed British primatologist, ethnologist, anthropologist, and United Nations Messenger of Peace) was asked a question: "Why did she do what she did for the chimps she has advocated for all her life?" She answered by sharing a true story.

A captive lab chimp had never lived outside a cage his entire life. Now freed by Jane and her team of researchers and scientists, the frightened primate sat and watched the other chimps in a large zoo compound—free of cages and with grassy, rocky, chimp-appealing offerings, including the sight and sound of others like him. He was terrified by such a contrast—from darkness to light.

A growing crowd of onlookers watched silently as the terrified chimp acclimated to his new world, and then in a united gasp of disbelief witnessed the chimp run and fall into the watery moat surrounding the enclosure. Not knowing what to do, never having experienced being in water before, he began to flail in terror and sink.

At that, a man in the crowd instantly jumped over the railing, dove into the water, and pulled the huge ape up and out of the water to safer ground. The man was even able to get there faster than the watching zookeeper, who was horrified, as were all the onlookers. The man made sure that the chimp was breathing all right. Climbing over the railing back to the crowd, he turned to see the chimp yet again running in fright and falling back into the water. Again, the man jumped over the railing, lifted the heavy, flailing chimp back up onto the grassy enclosure, and waited until the chimp seemed to realize that he was home and calmed down.

After what seemed like an eternity, everyone observed the chimp being welcomed by the others in the troop, appearing safe at last. Finally, someone in the crowd turned to the man and asked him, "Why did you do that? What would compel you to risk being killed by a huge, drowning ape that could have easily mauled you in fear?" And the man said simply, "I looked into his eyes."

An animal's eyes have the power to speak a great language.

—MARTIN BUBER

We are all interconnected: people, animals, our environment.
When nature suffers, we suffer. And when
nature flourishes, we all flourish.

—DR. JANE GOODALL

I have a challenge I'd like you to ponder. What if you could discover an entirely unique way of looking at your life guided by some of Mother Nature's finest teachers? Seriously. I'm talking about seeing your challenges as strengths, setbacks as chances for new perspective, losses as gains, and heartache as healing? What if you could change the way you see your situation just by watching a rock or a pearl or an otter or a spider just do their thing? I'm here to tell you that it really is as simple as that. Strange, but true.

Nature has helped me see that being human is, well, a natural thing. In order to find the answers we seek, we really don't have to go very far. In fact, the answers are there for us everywhere we go, in everything we see in the natural world.

It seems so much of what I've learned and continue to learn is through nature. Every leaf, every rock, every wave, every insect, every change of season--all of it has a message. Many of these messages have come to me through animals, but as you will see in this book, the messengers have also taken on many guises one wouldn't necessarily expect to find in a master teacher.

I, like the majority of earthlings, have hurdled over and slammed into thousands of individual courses. After all, that's what Earth School is all about. Learning, growing, falling over, getting up off the floor, and starting over again. We get dirty. We find ourselves knee-high in messes we created or somehow wallowed into. It's all around us. It's the joy and the horror of being alive.

But essential to our daily curriculum in Earth School are the teachers. Some cause us to smile when we remember their goodness and warm impact on our lives. Others were so cruel we can barely say their names or even dare to conjure up their image in our mind's eye. The teachers of our lives come in all packages; they are family members, lovers, life partners, neighbors, coworkers, mentors, strangers in passing, the homeless, the privileged, educators, animals, insects, flora and fauna everywhere, and on and on. They're all part of this life tapestry we bumble about in as human beings.

I've been touched by all of these teachers and more. Some have left deep, emotional scars; others have given me immeasurable gifts. All have pushed me further along my path.

The Nature Teachers are my most favorite. They have appeared to me on my daily walks outside my door as well as along the ocean and river, in my forest escapes to the mountains and rivers, or simply sitting under a tree or gazing out a window. They are an unlikely faculty, the likes of which one never expects to find in any kind of educational system. But when I finally stopped my own inner spinning long enough to breathe, I saw them. I watched and listened to them. I allowed them to teach me huge lessons. Now, whenever I find myself listing off the track, I make an effort to seek out these high masters and other new ones who appear constantly, and remember once again. All of them, in one way or another, guide me in different ways back to my better, stronger self, ultimately to use everything in my life as enrichment for my inner garden, growing all the power and love and validation I seek. Nature helps me understand and accept my humanness and know that all I wish for has always been there, alive within the seeds of my own soul.

I encourage you to find your connectedness and peace as you gather Strength from these Nature Teachers. I have cited but a few of them within this book. There's an infinite amount of them everywhere within the natural world. If you listen and watch, they will show you how very easy it is to thrive in spite of or because of—the challenges on your path. And once you "look into the eyes and souls" of all species, it is impossible to look away. Each of us is a living link to the heartbeat of life. We are truly One.

At some point in life, the world's beauty becomes enough.

—TONI MORRISON

I believe the world is incomprehensively beautiful.
An endless prospect of magic and wonder.

—ANSEL ADAMS

All plants are our brothers and sisters. They talk to us and if we listen, we can hear them.

-ARAPAHO

CHAPTER 1

THE STONE AND THE RIPPLE EFFECT

Kind words can warm three winters, while harsh
words can chill even in the heat of summer.

—CHINESE PROVERB

YEARS AGO, WHEN my son Jesse and I were tromping in the snow together in a little mountaintop town, we found ourselves ultimately standing by a near-frozen lake. It was hypnotic in its stillness, soft shards of ice gathering a winter crust above it, yet there were still great places of quiet water peering through. Jesse and I began tossing small stones into the watery pools and watched one by one the ripples that emanated from them in ever-widening circles.

Fascinated by how immediately and expansively the circles radiated with each stone toss, Jesse and I sat on a log and commented on the impact that this innocent activity had on both of us. Jesse, who was around eight at the time, found the lesson in what we had experienced right away. Just one little stone could cause a tremendous ripple effect. Good or bad, it is all in our own hands and intentions. We are each a little stone, and the ripples that we cause change us as they change others.

What we choose to believe and how we communicate it causes ripples of effect. Love or hate. Acceptance or rejection. Bigotry. Racism. Sexism. Anti-Semitism. Laughter. Sorrow. Energy. Exhaustion. You can uplift someone immediately with a kind word. Or destroy someone just as fast with a cruel one. You have the power. Oftentimes that power starts with a smile.

THE POWER OF A SMILE

Sometimes your joy is the source of your smile, but sometimes your smile can be the source of your joy.

—THICH NHAT HANH

There is actually a theory by notable scientists, researchers, and doctors that, as D.A. Bernstein, PhD, says, "Feedback from your face affects your emotional expression, mood, and behaviors." Dr. Bernstein says that even when you play-act anger and make a fierce expression, this will affect your internal sense of well-being. The angry expression that you telegraph on your face will trigger your amygdala, the emotional operating structure of your brain. If you put on a silly face, it will activate your pleasure center. Pretty amazing, isn't it?

A smile—a genuine, ear-to-ear, nothing phony-about-it smile—is like magic to your well-being. By smiling, you're actually helping your entire nervous and immune systems improve their level of effectiveness—and that means lowering your stress level, blood pressure, heart rate, and respiration, controlling and reducing fear-worry responses, and a whole lot more. Just a good old-fashioned smile can do all that.

Michael J. Hurd, PhD (www.drhurd.com), says, "Some people have told me that when they force a smile under difficult circumstances, they actually start to feel better. Individuals who feel nervous about public speaking will smile in order to appear confident. The result is a more comfortable feeling as they make their presentations. People with phobias are sometimes helped by trying to smile and laugh during the feared situation. Smiling unleashes the power to 'self-fulfill' a happy prophecy. Everybody knows that smiling, like happiness and calmness, can't be totally forced or faked. But maybe a little extra effort can perk up your emotional state, as well as improve the dynamics of your personal and business relationships. Give it a try! You can make a difference in the lives of everyone around you—one smile at a time."

Dr. Masaru Emoto, who was an internationally renowned science researcher and author, wrote a revolutionary series of books, the first one entitled *Messages from Water*. The premise of his research was that the power of prayer, beneficial healing sounds, and words can even change the physical property of water crystals. In his research, Dr. Emoto discovered that all substances and phenomena have their own unique magnetic resonance field. His photographs of the dramatic contrast between frozen water before and after prayer, angry and kind words or thoughts, and gentle and strident music are amazing. His work is so important on so many levels. He documented scientific evidence that all of life is a vital force capable of reacting to positive or negative energy. Everything. The more we are aware of this vital energy, the more we are able to focus on our own power and the impact it has on everything and everybody.

To this day, after each of my talks, I provide a basket of smooth, round stones for everyone in the audience. The stones are small reminders of our own unique energy. We each have the ability to change the world, shift molecules and perspective immediately positively or negatively. How we think and act and what or how we communicate can and does alter states of being. These ripples of effect happen moment-by-moment, day by day. Everything we do and say and think and feel sends ripples out to the world. We are each our own stone that is capable of creating mighty outcomes.

Jesse, now a grown man, often carries a special smooth stone with him wherever he goes. It gives him a sense of grounding, a true touchstone connecting to his higher self and acting as a reminder of the place and experience where he discovered that very stone. In time, he replaces the stone with another as he goes along his life journey. Each one contains its own energy and represents a kind of stepping-stone, reminding him of his forward climb.

My gift to you: find a stone and make it your own. And be mindful of the ripple effect you have—on friends, on children, on animals, on partners, on everyone you are in contact with in one way or another. Your words, thoughts, and actions are all powerful tools—of love or hate. Use them wisely.

When words are both true and kind,
they can change our world.

—BUDDHA

LESSON FROM THE STONE TEACHER:

I am the stone. My words, my actions, my heartfelt wishes,
my passions send out ripples of energy to the world when
splashed into water. I am powerful enough to impact
my own life and others' lives positively or negatively.

CHAPTER 2

THE PEARL

A pearl is a beautiful thing that is produced by an injured life. It is the tear [that results] from the injury of the oyster. The treasure of our being in this world is also produced by injured life. If we had not been wounded, if we had not been injured, then we will not produce the pearl.

—STEPHAN HOELLER

THOUGH I HAVEN'T actually cracked open any clams, oysters, or abalones to find pearls, I do love the metaphor attached to the creation of those incandescent gemstones. It seems natural to include it here as another Teacher.

Whenever I'm in a funk, wondering why I'm being burdened by something in my life, I think of the pearl. What creates such a precious work of art? Actually, a pearl doesn't start out that way. It begins as an irritant. Something annoying, a foreign piece of matter inside a mollusk. Maybe it's a grain of sand, some kind of parasite, or a human-devised object. Whatever it is, it's irritating in some way to the shellfish. So what happens? In order to protect its sensitive soft inner tissues, the sea animal isolates the irritant by slowly coating it with a kind of lustrous substance called nacre. We know it as mother-of-pearl. Layer after layer, the irritant is covered with this shiny buffering material until, in time, the result is a breathtaking pearl.

Knowing how a pearl is created has helped me put into perspective the many unseemly annoyances and irritants about myself and the challenges that slam into me daily. If I acknowledge them, layer them beautifully with positive energy--indeed, gift-wrap them and keep them in my life without being daunted by them—something so much better grows out of the process. I don't run away from the mess; I just use it, like compost, or clay and mud, to build and create something wonderful.

So whether your irritant is a small annoyance, such as dealing with personality clashes or awkward situations or situations dumped onto you without your approval, or your annoyance is a big one, such as bullying, homophobia, bigotry, racism, anti-Semitism, cruelty of any kind, health/addiction challenges, or tremendous losses, you still have the potential for pearl-power. (Now say *that* over and over again!)

Think about those annoyances, setbacks, and so on in your own life that can become beautifully luminescent if you give them time to heal and grow. It's amazing how they appear before you if you step back and truly see with your entire being and not with tunnel vision.

Everything that irritates us about others can
lead to an understanding of ourselves.

—CARL JUNG

LESSON FROM THE PEARL TEACHER:

I am the pearl. Oftentimes, it is the gritty, rough, edgy,
hard, and irritating situations in life that ultimately
birth beautiful results—if we take the time to
accept them and let them become so.

I go to nature to be soothed and healed,
and to have my senses in order.

—JOHN BURROUGHS

CHAPTER 3

THE ROCK AND THE WAVES

In the midst of winter, I finally learned that there was in me an invincible summer.

—ALBERT CAMUS

THE ROCK

SOME TIME AGO, on my daily walks by the ocean, I could see it looming amid the waves—a mighty rock. It's the kind of rock that--if he could get to it--my son, Ethan would straddle in a nanosecond. Ethan is a natural mountain climber, and for as long as I can remember, he could never resist the allure of such a welcoming, rocky challenge. Nature's craggiest, most dangerously beautiful heights and daring obstacles continue to capture his longing to straddle the edge. His startling black-and-white photographs, videos, and documentaries help me understand and see what draws him there—just like that rock I stood on before.

It remains alone, far from the shore, remote and unobtainable by human intruders. Still, it is close enough for me to appreciate its beauty

8

and the hundreds of convolutions, creases, and curves that wend their way through its surface. Sometimes it looks like the visage of a wizened Native American chieftain. Other times it looks like a craggy condominium for sea urchins and shore birds all moving in counterpoint to the stillness of the massive foundation beneath them. Then again, it's a diamond in the rough. Unpolished, unremarkable in its dark nondazzle, yet filled with hundreds of interesting facets and angles and corners.

There is a mystery about the rock. Is it the top of an ancient mountain still tucked deep within the watery depths? A hefty shard chipped off from a prehistoric earthquake or volcano? What are the millions of time passages it has witnessed? Pirate shipwrecks. Native rituals and seaside gatherings. Cataclysmic changes in weather. Lovers. Weddings. Funerals. Wildlife birds and mammals resting, birthing, mating, dying, feeding. This rock has seen and felt it all, and yet it's not talking. Life's secrets remain within it. And it simply rocks on.

Time after time I faced that rock. I watched it as I was bundled like an Eskimo from the cold—all scarves and collars zipped tight. Other times I stood soaked from an unexpected burst of rain and needed to wipe the heavy mist of droplets off my face. When the sun appeared again, I embraced the welcome warmth, enjoying the heat baking my head and back like a chummy embrace. And I saw how the rock weathers all these changes. How sparkly it looks on a quiet, full-moon night. How enduring it appears when huge waves pound and recede over and over again on and over it—the foamy filigree bubbling around it like a dancer's tutu.

Then there are moments when the water is so still it's barely audible. The ocean becomes transformed into a vast, unmoving lake as the tide slides away, revealing even more of the rock and the little creatures that live on its lower level. The changes seem to reflect or parallel my own high and low life tides. Maybe, I wonder, we are more connected to the gravitational biorhythms than we are even aware.

But through all these seasons and transformations from light to dark, high to low tide, winter to summer, the rock never varies. It remains stoic and beautiful and accepting. Oh, it may be slowly eroding away, but its subtle shedding is not visible. From my perspective, nothing seems to change its stance.

Over the years, its lesson has resonated within me. In time, I've found great solace in identifying with it. If I am my own rock, then there is a stillness within me. There is a peace. There is the ability to experience the waves of whatever my life is hit with, whatever washes over me, yet I don't lose myself in these waves. I remain. This doesn't mean I am impervious to life. I can feel the cold and the warmth and the joy and the sorrow and the ugly and the beautiful. But I am not any of those things, good or bad. I am simply who I am.

THE WAVES

Equally, I found many lessons in the waves. Deciding ultimately to personalize them, I began to see them as representing the challenges I had faced in the past and some that I face in the present, day-by-day, moment-to-moment.

Soon, I realized that the waves of divorce that devastated me were only waves. I was not the divorce. Nor was I the bankruptcy. Nor was I the loss of all the material possessions that I loved—the house and furniture and everything that filled that former world. They washed away, wave after wave. Yet I still remained. I didn't lose myself in them. I was there to experience them and to let them flow and go. Until other waves of life filled all the facets of my beingness.

I now find that when I begin to spin out-of-control, feel myself slipping, exhausted, full of fear or depression, holding on too tight, I have become the waves. I've forgotten my rockness. I've become other people's angst or energy or demands or ideas of who I am or should be. I've become life's labels, bills, debts, invitations, rejections, acceptance, addiction, abandonment, aging, opinions, too much analyzing. I've accepted fear. I have abandoned all that I am for the passionate temptation and allure of the waves.

This is not to denigrate the wonder of waves. Not at all. They're to be felt and experienced as an integral part of life. So we can and must feel passion. And love. And joy and laughter and delight and sorrow and all the precious and terrible feelings that move us further along our path. We just don't have to lose ourselves in them. When we remain strong within ourselves, we don't smother others--we don't make them or anything more important than ourselves. We don't get lost in the darkness or the light. We attract more power and appreciation and respect and trust and love from the world, because we are a steady, calm, solid force. We're not looking outward for approval. We're not needy. Indeed, we don't need anything, because we're comfortable in our own selves. And that's the foundation upon which true, deep, steady love and harmony can grow and rest and thrive.

I have discovered that it's only when I stop and focus back on me that I'm truly home. I'm learning to breathe deeply and relax my shoulders, as my tai chi teachers have taught me to do, no matter what is going on around me—other people's drama, an animated conversation or meeting, a party, whatever.

I settle into my bones and gather my own strength and energy. I appreciate all the waves that dance around me and even participate in them, but I'm doing all I can not to get lost in any of them. I remind myself that I am always and will forever be the rock.

What is joy without sorrow? What is success without failure? What is a win without a loss? What is health without illness? You have to experience each if you are to appreciate the other. There is always going to be suffering. It's how you look at your suffering, how you deal with it, that will define you.

—MARK TWAIN

11

LESSON FROM THE ROCK TEACHER:

When I see myself as a steady rock, I can accept all of life's
challenges. I feel them each in every way, but never lose
myself in any of them. No matter what I experience, good
and bad, I remain aware of my own style and pace and
place, comfortable and strong and beautiful being me.

LESSON FROM THE WAVE TEACHER:

When I see myself as the wave, I realize that I am all
about reacting to the world around me—the seasons, the
weather, the time of day and night, the pull of the tide,
all exterior dramas, all the joys and sorrows of life. There
is nothing to hold me still, to hold me back, to make me
remain the same. I am flux and flow and mercurial.

THE OTTER

Obstacles don't have to stop you. If you run into a
wall, don't turn around and give up. Figure out how
to climb it, go through it, or work around it.

—MICHAEL JORDAN

IT DOESN'T MATTER how many times we see them in the ocean, we all seem to get excited. "Wait, that's not a log! No, no, it's not kelp and it's not a seal! Look, it's an otter!" Fingers point. Binoculars focus in. Children are lifted up on shoulders to see them better. Joggers even stop running for a moment to smile at the brief water show. Everyone wants to watch otters.

Everything about the little furry creatures seems to inspire delight. Their endearing faces look like little Ewoks straight out of a Star Wars movie, with their permanent cuteness and a childlike demeanor of fur and flippers. You can see them bobbing along the ocean on their backs, pounding away on flipper-held rocks as they pry open the hard shells of sea urchins, snails, clams, mussels, abalone, crabs, and an ocean full of some forty types of marine species. At night you can hear the popping and breaking of shells as the little fur balls splash, and dine along the coast.

The crafty little critters are the only mammals other than primates known to use tools. Their whole bodies are made for a permanent life in the sea. They use their extendable front claws to get a better grip on spiny urchins and slippery fish. Their back paws are flipper-like and webbed to the very tips of their toes. One long toe on the outside of each back paw helps them swim better, but makes a tromp on land pretty challenging. They can weather their icy-cold home as well as they do because of all the creatures in the entire animal kingdom, sea otters have the thickest fur. The fur is air-filled, allowing them to float with ease high above the water. But there's no buffering blubber beneath that thick fur. So if any substance, like oil, coats it, the otter could die from exposure or from cold.

These little sea weasels captivate me, not only because of their cuteness, but mainly their resiliency. Time and time again, I have watched as they bob up and down, up and down above the rolling ocean beneath them. No matter how fearsome the waves appear as they build to a mighty peak and crash to the shore, otters continue their back-floating course seemingly undaunted by the drama. They just bob on. If one gets too close to jagged rocks or rocky shore, it quickly flips over on its belly and dives back to its "home zone," the comfort of deeper water and the thick kelp beds where otters anchor themselves to feed and sleep and breed and birth.

I remember years ago, I was river rafting with my family. Holding on for dear life, I white-knuckled the upcoming water ride, ultimately finding myself completely catapulted into the rocky roar of water. Nearly drowning, I was wholly terrified. The guide had warned me, though. He told me not to hold on, but rather to relax. I was too frightened to listen to him.

I was drenched and shivering and plopped back into the raft, and the guide again told me to let go of the sides of the boat when the next rapids hit. He said that if I just relaxed through it all, I wouldn't be dumped. He was right. I forced myself to trust the ride, the flow of the wild waters bucking me like a rodeo clown, and voila! I made it.

The bunch of us were now eased into the most peaceful, watery silence—an eddy of ease in counterbalance to our previous rough ride. All were high-fiving one another and beaming—and then in the distance we heard it ever so faintly. More rapids. I breathed deeply and made sure my hands weren't gripping the sides. The only way I was going to get through it was to trust the journey and relax through the rapids. I remember thinking, "Isn't this what life's all about?" I couldn't help remembering the words, "Let go. Let God."

Such it was, I realized, with otters. They appear to be laughing, kicking back, totally accepting their world of wild waves and impending doom. The threatening rocks surround them, but the otters don't crash into them, nor do they drown in the huge waves. They bob. When the rocks appear too close, the otters simply swim away. Or find some delicious delicacy in their midst. They don't seem to mind the ominous presence of obstacles anywhere on their paths. They even seem to delight in them. We can see all the scary possibilities from our vantagepoint, but the otter continues munching away on its miniscule meals.

I have found such grace, such a sense of peace in how this little animal weathers life. It lives with danger everywhere, yet it copes beautifully. Indeed, if it weren't for human encroachment and mysterious, debilitating diseases that continue to endanger the lives of these innocent beings, I truly believe they would be unstoppable. Otters are tough little water warriors in every way. They have taught me much.

Always behave like a duck—keep calm
and unruffled on the surface,
but paddle like the devil underneath.

—Lord Barbizon

LESSON FROM THE OTTER TEACHER:

There are challenges, obstacles, daunting situations everywhere we go on various occasions or in moments in our lives.
Often, there is nothing we can do to change them. We can only
change our way of dealing with them, change our perspective,
change our course, ride above them, go with the flow, find re-
newed strength within ourselves because of them, let go of fear,
and feed our higher selves while living with whatever looms on
our path. We can use these fearsome situations as boundar-
ies as well as opportunities, knowing that when they appear,
greener pastures or more comforting waters are just beyond.
All we need to do is relax and seek our inner "home zones."
They are always there.

CHAPTER 5

THE SPIDER

Great things are not done by impulse, but by a
series of small things brought together.

—Vincent van Gogh

I sat and soaked up the soothing sulfur hot spring. Felt the hot squish of mud beneath my toes, and then leaned against a comfortable rock as I watched the midday light dapple through the pine forest. That's when I saw a glint of something from a branch overhead. Looking closer, I could see it was a silk strand connected to the most intricate weavings of other strands, creating a mandala of sparkling lines and circles. A spider's web. A masterpiece of geometric beauty.

The web lifted and lowered ever so slightly, seeming to breathe with the morning breeze. Above it, busily extending her life's work ever larger, circle by circle, was the spider. The silk lines eased their way out of her spinnerets as she moved effortlessly back and forth, the tips of her eight legs moist with oil, preventing her from getting trapped within her own web. Each silk strand was, weight for weight, stronger than steel, yet appeared to be like fairy dust—light and dazzling against the dark greens and browns of the towering trees.

At last, her creation was finished, and she balanced silently on a strand waiting, waiting. I watched. Like a cat ready to pounce, she didn't move. Everything about her was still, and yet I could almost feel her bottled energy, her state of keen readiness. Everything, her entire existence, was designed for this moment. For in an instant, a hapless insect could fly into her webby trap and the arachnid would instantly have her take-out (or rather take-in) meal.

After a few hours of sulfur-soaking with my friends, I was ready to leave. But in all that time, the spider never moved from her vantage point. She continued that silent vigil next to her gossamer trap in the woods.

I marveled at her work of art, and most of all the gifts she gave me, the wonders of patience and tenacity. That spider was a study in vibrant stillness. No one was around to cheer her on or give her reason to believe that she would even succeed. There didn't seem to be a glut of insects in the area she had chosen for her web. But still, she picked that place for some reason known only to her, and she waited for it to pay off. She might have waited hours for sustenance—maybe days, for all I know. But she did everything she was born to do in that predatory moment. It was a singular, magical, intricate study of doing the best you can using your gifts, trusting your own unique talents, and then letting go of the outcome.

It might not always work out the way one plans. I mean, a person could tromp through the brush and whack the web apart, completely oblivious to the damage he caused. Or a storm could kick up and the wind and rain and falling branches and leaves could rip her meticulous work to smithereens. And then what would that spider do? Start all over again. Maybe in another, safer part of the forest, near a cave or a rocky crevasse. Perhaps exactly at that same place after the storm died down and the sun came out and more insects were flushed from their hiding places. Another web would be woven to trap the next batch.

I'm reminded of the exquisite works of the artist Andy Goldsworthy, as seen in his documentary, *Rivers and Tides,* as well as in his extensive collection of books. If you haven't seen this film or his books, you are missing out on a modern-day genius.

What is so transfixing about Goldsworthy's creations is that they are temporary, as ephemeral as life. Each one is created from nature, born from the world of rocks and leaves and ice and earth, sand, snow, and sticks. He weaves them into intricate patterns, towering, swirling, majestic works of art. But they ultimately succumb to rivers and tides, wind and weather, the seasons themselves, as each Goldsworthy masterpiece eventually floats or blows or plummets away, overpowered by the power of nature. All that remain are the images preserved forever in film and photos.

What you learn from watching this artist is that it is the moment of creation, the work itself, that matters. Not tomorrow. Not the next day or the day after that. All that matters is the very moment—the patience and time and attention and vision that he puts into each piece. His works are the epitome of Eckhart Tolle's incredible book *The Power of Now.* For all that truly matters is the very moment we are in.

So it is with the spider and her web. The ravages of nature and the fragility of chance don't seem to deter her from focusing on the moment and the ultimate purpose of food-trapping. No matter what, she simply starts all over again, weaving, connecting, spinning her silk trap with the same perpetual patience and tenacity. I have much to learn from witnessing such single-minded mastery.

LESSON FROM THE SPIDER TEACHER:

I can orchestrate each moment for my highest good, using the gifts of patience, perseverance, and inventiveness to get the job done. The outcome may not be as I planned, but no matter what happens as the result of my efforts, I can both let go and start all over again. I am not fragile. I am resilient. And no matter how hard I work to create a specific result, I know that the element of surprise can undo it all. Starting over is an integral part of starting.

*Perseverance is failing nineteen times
and succeeding the twentieth.*

—JULIE ANDREWS

CHAPTER 6

THE RIVER

I would love to live like a river flows, carried
by the surprise of its own unfolding.

—John O'Donohue

I SAW IT from the pass way above the highway as we rounded the corner in our car. We could see it snake and stretch far below for miles within the rocky ravine, cushioned by acres of verdant forest and mountain trails. The river. I'd been longing to see it ever since I moved away from the comfortable little world I'd created just inches from my beloved ocean. Time and circumstances beckoned me to continue on my path, and I had to let go and trust. Though there were some very good aspects to all of it—in particular, finally being with my love, Pete, on a full-time basis—but I still wasn't happy about the dramatic change of scenery.

Why did change have to happen? Why couldn't things stay the same? Why, when everything seemed so perfect, was I catapulted to parts unknown? I didn't have the answers to any of these questions, but I knew that I needed to be near moving, rushing, bubbling water to help center my soul. I practically ran to her side the minute we parked the car.

While Pete began his own solitary centering of riverside exploration, I sat barefoot on the river's edge and eased my toes into the icy ballet of bubbles and swirls.

The words "—you can't step into the same river twice" began playing in my mind over and over again. "Why the hell not?" I shouted back to whoever so smugly decided such a thing. What was change all about, anyway? This was the same river everyone had been talking about since the beginning of time. It hadn't changed. But then the voice whispered deep within my soul as it always does, "Just watch…"

And so I did. I watched the river being a river. I saw a stick from far down in a quiet little eddy wend its way through a whirl to rest in a patch of calm and then circle away the next instant, pulled by the laughing waters. I watched as whitecaps played on the surface one moment, and all was rush and passion and splashing, and then, in a breath, all was still and the water receded and calmed itself. And so it would go—in one instant, trickles would build into waves hiding rocks, crashing into boulders, and rolling tiny twigs and pebbles around and around, dancing leaves across it, and then the next moment, it would ramp down, slowing and babbling softly like a lullaby, as if, for a second, it suddenly decided to be a lake. It never did the same thing again. It never sounded the same. Over and over, as fast as a breath inhaled and exhaled, the river changed before my eyes and ears. What I'd perceived as one big thing was actually a kaleidoscope of lots of little things—sounds and sights changing, changing, ever changing. I'd never seen it that way. In fact, I'd never really seen it at all.

Such was *my* life, I realized, as I continued my river watch. Everything, no matter how fixed or permanent it appears, is in a state of flux: one moment it's one way, and the next, another. Too often throughout my journeys, I would settle into a false sense of security. Once I began to cozy into the life I'd gathered around me, one-by-one little blankets would be taken away or get lost in the shuffle. Some blanket losses wouldn't even be discernable. They might have been the teensiest of coverlets. And since I was still feeling cozy, I wouldn't notice their absence. But when the big quilts and afghans and comforters began slipping away, I suddenly noticed that I was feeling cold. Actually, I was at that temperature for quite a while. It didn't happen overnight. I just was made aware of the change. "What in the hell happened to all my blankets?" I would shout through blue lips, my body quivering at the freezing point. That was when I was finally forced to start over and give myself new comfort, blanket-by-blanket.

Slowly, I'm learning to not settle down or into anything, but rather ease into a new situation, commit to the lessons and experiences of it, really savor it, watch it, listen to it with my entire being—but not lose myself in any of it. If we really stay in the present and stay aware, we see or hear or smell or taste or feel the changes that transpire moment by-moment. If we cannot see through our eyes, if we are blind, then we must depend on our other senses to know our surroundings. The same for loss of hearing. Or moving. Or speaking. We must feel the changes within and those surrounding us. That is how we must see the world we are in—with all of our being, with the senses that work for us. And when we do that, we discover that nothing stays the same. And that change is as integral to life as is breathing.

Change is not merely necessary to life. It is life.

—ALVIN TOFFLER

The reality is that we are literally changing all the time. Our own planet is swirling on its axis, rotating every twenty-four hours, revolving around the sun once every 365 days. But there is a great deal of flux within that evolution. The amount of energy that the earth receives from the sun isn't always the same. Changes in the sun and changes in the earth's orbit around it influence this energy intake. The changes are boundless: the weather, the seasons, day to night, natural disasters—earthquakes, tsunamis, volcanoes, forest fires, tornadoes, avalanches, hurricanes, droughts, floods, storms, gluts of insects, endless ecosystem imbalance, the melting of glaciers and icebergs, the wrenching extinction of interminable numbers of species, on and on as we witness the staggering destruction caused by global warming. Change can be devastating, but in time—maybe even decades or eons from now—it can also be the key to expansion and renewal.

Even our bodies go through transformation of some kind day-by-day, internally and externally. Old cells give way to new ones over and over again. We always have a second chance to renew ourselves. Take our skin, for example. As we move about, our old skin cells get rubbed and worn away, pushed to the surface by new cells. In fact, every single minute, thirty to forty thousand dead skin cells fall away from our bodies. In a matter of one month, our entire bodies have created a brand-new layer of skin cells. We can literally say we're not the same person minute-by-minute, month-to-month! We shed our skins along with others, too—spiders and lobsters, many reptiles, plants, trees, and a whole planet full of flora and fauna that regenerate in order to grow. The butterfly becomes a butterfly through a series of changes—egg to caterpillar to chrysalis—before it emerges and spreads its brilliance in the sunlight. The drama of living and dying is played out daily in all forms of life.

I had to think this over. If all of life is forever moving atoms about, rearranging itself in infinitesimal ways, why would I think my life is any different? Am I not going against my own grain by holding on so tight? Isn't "normal" a state of release and letting go, even within the confines of a seemingly solid foundation of familiarity? Watching the river helped me understand even more why I need to let go of my past and flow into the new present. By holding on tight-fisted to a past that no longer exists, my own inner soul river, I'm simply damming it. I'm stopping the flow. I could even drown in it.

Now, when I return to visit my old haunts, I see that nothing is the same. Though my close friends are still and will always be my close friends no matter what the distance is between us, our immediate dynamic has changed, because we don't live physically near one another. Someone else is living in the place I once called home. A new energy has transpired on my street, at my old job, on the path I used to walk along by the sea. It might all look the same at first glance, but it has changed. It had to. Why? Because I've changed. Because change is part of life. That's why we can't step into the same place twice. As the author Thomas Wolfe said, we can't go home again to the same experiences. Life goes on, and so should we—savoring its beauty and passion and peace and depth and shallowness and resonance and silence. We need to see ourselves just like the river—as a vital, living, breathing, evolving force that is changing every second, along with everything around us.

Live life like a loose garment.

—ANONYMOUS

LESSON FROM THE RIVER TEACHER:

Nothing ever stays the same; all of life, including our own bodies, is a moving, breathing, changing presence. In order to cherish it, grow, and learn from it, truly love all that it is, we must not hold onto it, hold it back, dam it up in any way. Life is to be experienced in the very moment we experience it. All of life moves within and around us. It is not static. It is not the same, ever. Everything is flux and flow, and so are we.

Seek out a tree and let it teach you stillness

—ECKHART TOLLE

*In nature nothing is perfect and everything
is perfect. Trees can be contorted,
bent in weird ways, and they're still beautiful.*

—ALICE WALKER

Trees are poems that the earth writes upon the sky.

—KAHLIL GIBRAN

Trees are sanctuaries. Whoever knows how to speak to them, whoever knows how to listen to them, can learn the truth. They do not preach learning and precepts, they preach, undeterred by particulars, the ancient law of life.

—HERMAN HESSE

CHAPTER 7

THE ASPEN

Maybe you are searching among branches
for what only appears in the roots.

—RUMI

I'VE ALWAYS BEEN so drawn to them—aspen trees. Their beauty bedazzles. You have to stop and stare. On our travels to the rocky majesty of Crested Butte, Aspen, and Vail, Colorado, Pete and I did just that, drawn to look closer and take photos of what we had long ago discovered about them: these gorgeous groves are connected by one single seedling spread by root suckers! Brand-new stems in the colony appear from 98 to 130 feet from the parent tree.

Pointing the camera at their legendary roots, I saw for myself the wonder of their reputation. Entwined together, as if holding hands, were rows upon rows of gnarly root systems one disappearing into the grasp of the next one beside it. You could barely tell which root belonged to which tree. It all seemed like one continuous extension reaching out to the next.

If left untouched, each individual tree can actually live for 40 to 150 years aboveground, but it is this astounding root system of the colony that is so long-lived. There are cases where such root systems thrive for thousands of years, sending up new trunks as the older trunks wither and die off aboveground.

One famous colony grows in Utah and has been given the name Pando (Latin for "I spread"). This colony is also known as the Trembling Giant and is estimated to be eighty thousand years old, making it possibly the oldest living colony of aspens. Some aspen colonies become tremendously large with time, spreading over three feet per year, eventually covering acres of land. They're able to survive forest fires, because their roots are below the heat of the fire and new sprouts grow after the fire burns out. Plus aspen wood is not as flammable as the wood of other tree species. How amazing is that?

This tree is a survivor because of its resilience and strength—its very roots stand together in support of life's most daunting challenges. As we walked beside them, we noted that some of these gorgeous trees were twisted or bent. And that was attributed to the fact that they withstand the horrific pounding of mountain avalanches. The trees rarely break or splinter, but hold strong and manage to thrive in spite of gigantic snow beatings. They're even historically life-savers, containing salicylates, chemicals found in aspirin.

As a grove, aspens can and do withstand much in life that they wouldn't be able to handle as a singular entity. I know this is the reason why I love the aspen so much. Not only for its legendary golden beauty in the fall of each year, but also because it symbolizes what I wish the human species would realize. We are one and the same. Yes, each of us has our own patterns, styles, colors, languages, cultures, religions, and so on, but we are more the same than not. Our uniqueness—our branches and leaves—may set us apart, but our similarities connect us. We are born of the same root system, thriving from the same foundation of life that feeds and nurtures us all. We are one. Unfortunately, I believe we have become so focused on our differences that we have lost sight of our common ground.

The deepest level of communication is not communication, but communion. It is wordless...beyond speech...beyond concept.

—THOMAS MERTON

LESSON FROM THE APEN TEACHER:

Though we are individual, separate, and distinct beings, we still grow stronger by our support of and connection to one another. It is possible to live together in harmony anchored by the unity of strength in numbers, allowing one another to thrive, linked in a common ground of support.

And don't think the garden loses its ecstasy in winter. It's quiet, but the roots are down there riotous.

—RUMI

They are giving back the light they have been absorbing from the sun all summer.

—JOHN BURROUGHS

The moment you realize your bones are made from the same dust as the planets, your lungs breathing the air of migrating butterflies, and your blood is pumping because of the love and care of thousands, is when you realize you're not broken or alone as you think you are. You are full of the world.

—SOULSEEDS

CHAPTER 8

THE BUTTERFLY

The butterfly counts not months but
moments, and has time enough.

—RABINDRANATH TAGORE

KAIO'S MAMA, FABIANE, shouted for us to enjoy the delicate beauty of the little butterfly before it flew away. My grandson, Kaio (who was five-years-old at the time) and I ran over to witness the tiny beauty at our feet. None of us breathed as we watched her flap her wings and begin to take off, and then—and then she fluttered, swayed, and loop-de-looped lopsided backdown to earth. Oh! We gasped in unison. Something was terribly wrong.

Kaio looked at her closer. "Oh no, Nana! I see the problem. She's broken. There's a hole in her wings. She's hurt. I don't think she can fly!" Instantly, our joy at her jewel-like splendor dissolved into sorrow. Then we went into action. "Nana, butterflies like nectar!" I soaked a bit of bread with honey. But the stickiness looked like it was going to glue her to a fast albeit sweet demise. "I know!" Kaio brightened. "Flowers!" He and I ran to gather as many flowers as we could find, and he brought them to her. She rallied, showed a spirited attempt to climb upon them, and then again tried to fly away, only to find herself leveled, staggering to the earth far below her vertical goal of sky and treetops and clouds.

Kaio and I ran along beside her. We placed her in a generous earthen pot and filled it with more flowers, hoping she would find solace in a safe garden for her final resting place. But no. She tried over and over to fly, and fell and lifted and toppled over again. Kaio named her "Flower," and I marveled at her strong will to live even though everything about her was ragged and growing ever more weary. Her strength was ebbing. "Nana, I think she's going to die…"

We talked about how fierce she was in her fight for life. We worried that she might be grabbed up by a bird, or the dog might inadvertently step on her. So once again we scooped her up, placed her in a quiet grove of bushes, and brought her a tiny cup of passion fruit juice surrounded by more flowers, and there she rested. Exhausted. Probably from us carrying her about too much. In time, Kaio was off playing, his work with "Flower" over. Somehow I knew that he wisely knew there was not much more he could do for her and moved on.

But I couldn't leave her side. I watched as she tried to drink the sweet liquid while her wings opened and closed more and more slowly. In my heart I could almost feel the aching strains of Puccini's exquisite opera, *Madama Butterfly*. In moments, her wings finally closed together as if in prayer, transforming her into what looked like a minuscule Japanese origami—and at last she fell over on her side, nestling against the flowers.

I guess the greatest lesson that beautiful little Nature Teacher taught me was that life is experienced in moments—some longer, some briefer, but all moments. We can't hold onto them. We each have our own path, our own time limit. And we must live with all our might until our time is up. Until then, we mustn't give up.

That little butterfly was determined to fly until she simply couldn't anymore. I loved that about her. All we can do is offer one another loving support—maybe even a flower or two—moment-to-moment. That's more than enough.

What the caterpillar calls the end of the world the master calls a butterfly.

—RICHARD BACH

LESSON FROM THE BUTTERFLY TEACHER:

Time is limitless. We either have a lot of it or none at all. Before we know it, our time is up. But until that very moment of time-out, we must live as if the sky's the limit. We must keep on facing our challenges and dance, create, walk, run, dream, play, love until we can't anymore. Whole lifetimes are lived in increments—long or short. It takes courage to try to fly even if there are holes in our wings. The beauty and joy of intention set us free.

CHAPTER 9

THE WEED

*A weed is a plant that has mastered every survival skill
except for learning how to grow in rows.*

—Doug Larson

I HAVE FOUND that one of the most enduring Nature Teachers is not the most appreciated. In fact, for many, it's considered the cockroach of the plant kingdom. The weed.

I've never known why it is so hated, so completely undermined. For what I appreciate most about weeds is their determination to grow outside the lines. Yes, they wreak havoc inside coiffed gardens of landscaped perfection. But they don't seem to care. I imagine them laughing at their undesired presence as they emerge with their scruffy bedhead look, some rumpled and scraggly, others spiky and wild, and many with a beauty all their own. They stretch to the sky. They wear flowers and burrs and stickers. They spread and burst into places no one seems to want them to be—and, like the famous honey badger they simply don't give a shit.

You can pull them out. Poison the hell out of them. Swear at them. Find the perfect chemical solutions and fertilizers to deter them. But ultimately the weeds win. Once a garden is deserted, or a field is left to its own resources untended by human attention, weeds take over and make their untamed presence known. They grow anywhere, adapting to any situation. They don't seem to have any special requirements in order to do their thing or be who they are. They don't apologize. They just appear without any need for ceremony—happy to be alive wherever they grow. Rocky, deserted paths? They're thriving. Discarded hillsides? Trash-inundated ditches? Inside train tracks, cracks in the sidewalk, freeway embankments? There they are.

There's always a weed to be discovered, seemingly unaware of its marked "ugly duckling-ness." It bobs and dances in the sunshine and breezes, appearing more swan-like than not. I love what James Russell Lowell says about the weed, that it is truly "--no more than a flower in disguise, which is seen through at once, if love give a man eyes."

Because I believe that the weed has within it something most of us long for but don't have. Self-esteem. It's comfortable with itself. It has a beauty, joy, and resolve all its own no matter what the world says it is. I love weeds, and I strive to have all that they are and have—the fortitude of a cockroach and the elegance of a calla lily.

I didn't want to tell the tree or weed what it was.
I wanted it to tell me something and through
me express its meaning in nature.

—WYNN BULLOCK

LESSON FROM THE WEED TEACHER:

To embrace who we are in spite of our imperfections is the greatest gift we can give ourselves. Sometimes—more often than not—we show up and express ourselves in ways that don't fit what others might want us to be. But the goal is to be all right with simply being who we are no matter where we are, no matter what we do, no matter who shows up on our path and tries to redefine and conform us into ways that make them feel more comfortable. The goal is not only to accept our own selves, but to accept others as well. Within us all there is a scrappiness, a uniqueness, the freedom of "weed-ness" that must be honored and loved.

I believe that tomorrow is another day and I believe in miracles.

—AUDREY HEPBURN

CHAPTER 10

THE YAM

The sun shines not on us but in us.

—JOHN MUIR

I'D LEFT THE yam alone in the kitchen bowl for far too long. Plans to bake or cook or boil it had definitely passed, and now it was ready to be tomorrow's next garbage/compost addition. Then I noticed the little buds peeping out of it. Tiny leafy reminders seemed to shout at me, like the famous Monty Python quip, "I'm not dead yet!" And so it wasn't. The hearty tuber was very much alive and worthy of being appreciated, if not for a delicious meal, then certainly as a delicious work of natural beauty.

I placed it in a vase, added water, and settled it in the sunshine. And in just a matter of days, voila! It transformed into this viney wonder, spreading its loveliness out and over and above my kitchen sink. The little tuber completely exploded with sinewy greens winding all across the countertop, to my delight. And then after a year, it began to wane, its leaves yellowing and falling. It looked like the Grim Yam-Reaper had cast the final death knell.

I almost gave in and said my final good-byes—she'd had an amaz-ingly long run, after all. But then I stopped, thinking "Maybe there is more to this feisty tuber. Maybe I should give her one more shot." So I planted what looked like a rapidly shriveled shell of a yam with roots still intact but appearing about as done as a dead yam could look. I bought a pretty ceramic pot and filled it with rich, miracle-growing soil, watered her, and put her back in that same sunshiny place she seemed to like so much. And it worked. In a matter of days, there were new buds pop-ping out all over the place, and then more vines started breathing and stretching out. A new life began from the old one.

If there is such a thing as yam-reincarnation I was looking at it. And then I did the same thing with another tuber about to end it all. That one has taken over our kitchen, looking like something out of *Little Shop of Horrors*. The lesson learned? Never give up hope. There is a power within us all—all living beings—that when tended to and nurtured and given the time to be believed in and cared for grows strong. Mother Nature teaches us over and over again to trust that endings yield begin-nings—no matter how they may appear to us. Death is but a passage into new life. The final shell may disappear, but the spirit, the soul, the es-sence of that being does live on—like abundant green and joyous vines given another, transformative chance to be.

I wonder constantly at the spirit of those who are not only able to rise above the worst situations in the world, but who do so by saving others in endless ways as well. Humans and nonhumans do this all the time. I need this kind of reminder every minute. And so I am grateful for this lovely veggie still sprouting and smiling in the sunshine months after I thought it had faced its ultimate cessation. I couldn't help but wonder who had benefited the most from such a miraculous transition? But maybe it wasn't so unusual after all—beings of all species that have been rescued from the depths of misery more often than not rise like the phoenix from the ashes, ultimately saving those who thought they were saving them.

This Nature Teacher lesson has taught me to never give up. To nurture hope in the midst of what appears to be hopeless. We must always focus on the positive outcome, no matter what. That's what I learned from the words of Otto Frank, Anne Frank's father, during an especially hopeless time in my life. He wrote to me saying, "Even if the end of the world would be imminent you still plant a tree today." Of course he was right.

Miracles do not, in fact, break the laws of nature.

—C.S. Lewis

LESSON FROM THE YAM TEACHER:

Even if we believe we are on empty and have absolutely nothing left to give or receive, we still have an indomitable strength of will to thrive and shine. There is alive within us all a voice shouting to be heard: "I'm not dead yet!" It's that treasure, that gold mine glowing inside our souls wanting us to grow beyond our challenges that fuels us to take the time to nurture who we are. We're wired to live even if all looks hopeless and in counterpoint to what we think is so.

CHAPTER 11

THE PALM TREE

A tree that is unbending is easily broken.

—LAO TZU

I DON'T KNOW if it's the sound or the sight of them that I love most. From my vantage point, graceful palms dance in the blustery winds outside the windows. High above the ground, on the fourth floor of our San Diego apartment, we were at eye level to a glistening circle of these emerald beauties swaying in every view.

The shushing symphony of palm fronds and wind lulls me into a state of calmness. Boo and Scout curl into quiet *cat*-atonia next to me as we watch and listen to the palms leaning and bending in tune with the gusts of wind playing around them. Amazing, I find myself wondering, that they don't break in half.

What is it about them that makes them so malleable, yet so strong? Why don't they crack from such airborne pummeling time and time again? "It's their flexibility that contributes to their strength," Ted Safford, a certified arborist, explains in my phone conversation with him.

The Nature Teacher lesson resonated loud and clear. If palms were rigid and unyielding in structure, they would easily be felled by wild winds, "—but—" Safford continues, "—you see palm trees blowing and bending in hurricanes and horrific storms—and yes, some are downed by them, but in all my thirty-five years of maintaining palms, I've never seen one break."

In fact, research has proven that when palm trees are bent to such a degree that they're practically parallel to the ground from the challenging gusts, their root system actually gets stronger, initiating new opportunities for growth.

I learned that palm trees aren't really trees at all, but rather in the family of flowering plants—the only order of monocots called Arecales. Ted admits his great affection for palms is not only because of their supple acquiescence to treacherous weather, he loves their longitudinal simplicity. They don't have added baggage—heavy branches and leaves—to weigh them down. Palms lose their wind-resistant leaves a lot faster than trees lose their branches. Once the leaves are gone in a storm, there isn't much left to catch the wind.

Palm trees also have an extremely flexible, fibrous trunk and a shallow yet regenerative root system as compared to much sturdier trees, such as oak. This bendy ability gives the palm true mobility and windsway. The shallow, thinner roots make it easier for the palm not only fall to over rather than snap in half, but to rebuild a root structure yet again.

My goal now is to be more palm tree like in my approach to life. This is something that my tai chi teachers taught me as well. When someone is coming at you in a mighty attack and you stand rigid, you are easily pushed over. But when you relax your shoulders and move ever so slightly with the punch, the attacker is the one who falls. I've seen this happen over and over again in class.

Set patterns, incapable of adaptability, of
pliability, only offer a better cage.
Truth is outside of all patterns.

—BRUCE LEE

LESSON FROM THE PALM TREE TEACHER:

The best way to face adversity and the inevitable body slams of surprises, setbacks, and losses is to do it with the same grace and majesty of a palm tree and a tai chi master. To not stand rigid in fear and ultimately crack under pressure, but rather calm down in an inner dance-like sway to the wild winds of change. To not be blown away by situational storms, but relax into them and let your flexibility—your acceptance of life the way it *is,* not the way you wish it to be—ultimately be your strength.

CHAPTER 12

THE FLOWER POD AND THE WORM

Don't be afraid your life will end; be
afraid that it will never begin.

—GRACE HANSEN

PERIODICALLY ALONG MY daily walks, I find one lying on the path. Knocked off from its stem, separated from the rest of its floral family, a singular flower pod awaits its final ending. Kicked aside or simply left to wither in the hot sun, it rests, vulnerable and alone.

The same is true for a worm in its last curl about to crisp on the pavement. I tap it lightly, and if there's a bit of a wriggle left, I place it back into the grass and rich soil and watch as it begins to awaken into what appears to be a joyful lottery moment. For the worm and for me. Both happy to experience life in its most singular moment. This is what a last chance looks like. What appears as an ending has miraculously become a beginning, and it always delights me to know how truly happy I feel over this tiny act of grace. Who really rescues whom, after all?

I rarely can resist gathering up these little beings. The worm goes back into its earthy home and the pod goes back with me, where I then plop it into a cool glass of water. There, within minutes, I watch as it begins to slowly open—as if in surprise, having already accepted its doom and discovering there'd been a last-minute recall from its sidewalk sentencing. Petal-by-petal, it absorbs the soothing sunshine and fresh water, living in a glorious last gasp before its closing act.

I am forever awed by such bursts of life, for they teach me much not only about pod potential and worm renewal, but something more—a strong belief that we are wired to live. We all have the chance to tap into that pocket of vibrant energy tucked inside our cells and bring it forth. We must never give up hope. Little flower pods have powerful life forces in them. Worms do as well. Everything does. And so do we. Thrive on!

Nothing can dim the light which shines from within.

—MAYA ANGELOU

LESSON FROM THE FLOWER POD AND WORM TEACHERS:

We all have a profound strength within us to live and express ourselves—even when all appears hopeless. We might not believe it at the time, but if given a second chance to live, to express ourselves, to climb back up after falling down—even if for a brief burst of a moment—our spirits are equipped to rally and make it possible.

CHAPTER 13

THE CATS

Here comes the sun, here comes the sun,
And I say it's all right...

—GEORGE HARRISON

As I GREET the new day, flinging back blinds and opening windows, letting in the early light and fresh new morning breath, our cats, Boo and Scout, seek the first patches of sunshine streaking across the floor. They follow it at the sides of chairs and beds. Across the laptop. Next to the screen door. Filtering onto the carpet. Like mini heat-seekers, they pounce on the instant warmth that immediately puts them into a blissful Zen state of ecsta-z's.

Watching them, I can't help feeling a twinge of envy at how easily they seem to find what makes them happy and immerse themselves in it without a moment's hesitation. Why can't I be more cat-like and let myself enjoy the comforting pleasure of a simple patch of sun—even for a few minutes? Set aside all the shoulds and gotta do's and lists upon lists of all that I expect of myself to accomplish from dawn to dusk.

How good would it be to just allow myself the decadence of purposelessness? The tingling sensation of simply stretching and curling, rolling and yawning into a lazy clump—grabbing a small piece of early a.m. rays before they vanish from each room into the day like a bride gathering the silken train of her gown.

There are two means of refuge from the miseries of life: music and cats.

—ALBERT SCHWEITZER

Keep your face to the sunshine and you cannot see a shadow.

—HELEN KELLER

LESSON FROM THE CAT TEACHERS:

Comfort should be as easy to embrace as the way in which cats savor such peaceful *purr*suits. My two favorite Nature Teachers are teaching me to *paws* upon the instantaneous joy of radiant self-indulgence—one sunbeam at a time. Here comes the sun, indeed. It's all right to stretch and laze in the glow. It's more than all right. It's imperative.

Sunshine on my shoulders makes me happy.

—JOHN DENVER

C H A P T E R   1 4

THE BIRD

*It is our choices that show what we truly
are, far more than our abilities.*

—J. K. ROWLING

THE CATS WERE on it first. Poised in a *purr*manant stance dictated by some primordial instinct, they remained fixated and staring at the glass door of our balcony. There, on the other side of the night, pummeling the doors and windows in a frantic flutter back and forth, was a baby bird. Seemingly lost in the dark, drawn to the light beyond the glass, it slammed its little wings over and over again in a futile attempt to free itself from the nightmare.

The cats were hypnotized, following the wee bird's body slams from above and below their vantage points. What to do? Pete and I were prepared to find a way to capture the wayward baby and rescue it as fast as we could. And then, as if by magic, it stopped, turned around, and, shaking its wings in what appeared to us as triumph (possibly a birdy "aha" moment?), just flew away into the night.

Relief! Though the cats now had to resign themselves to the boredom of relinquishing their feline fascination with their version of "The Food Channel", Pete and I were thrilled to witness the little bird's freedom. That, and realizing the rest of our evening wouldn't have to be spent rescuing and succoring a tiny terrified feathered baby.

Later, we marveled at the drama that had broken through the peace of quietude, with cats splayed out contentedly around us as Pete and I played our guitars together. And then that "What the...?" broke the silence and nearly the glass door.

The next morning, we recalled our surprise at witnessing such heart-pounding drama. And it occurred to us that it was yet another Nature Teacher gift: the lesson of choice. I think I'll leave those smudge marks on the glass door and windows just a little longer to remember the impression that little bird made in lifting our own spirits as it lifted its wings and soared away.

If you do not change direction, you may
end up where you are heading.

—LAO TZU

LESSON FROM THE BIRD TEACHER:

Even if you think that what is before you is your demise, a wall
of impossibility, disappointment, and exhaustive dead ends,
most of the time all you have to do is turn around. Turn away
from it. Discover a new perspective that not only might save you,
mentally and/or physically, but even allow you to spread your
wings and fly in an entirely new and far more freeing direction.

CHAPTER 15

BLIND BIRDING BY THE BAY

I shut my eyes in order to see.

—PAUL GAUGUIN

THOSE WHO HAVE been brave enough to drive with me over the years probably still have fingernail-scars embedded in their palms from white-knuckling. I specialize in getting lost and rarely being found. I have no sense of direction. And I will never drive on a freeway again unless you put a gun to my head.

That should set the stage for a drive I did with one of the best and most patient navigators ever. Did I say that he was sight challenged, as in almost blind? True. A few years ago, I was directed through the San Diego traffic by my visually-challenged friend, Claude. A former biologist and birder, this amazing genius has socked away an inventory of facts—about flora and fauna and a whole lot more—in his brilliant brain. And one morning he offered to share his wisdom and memorized street sense with my friend Willie and me.

I picked him up at his home, whereupon he proceeded to kindly sense my inward breathing as I sucked in the stress of traversing my way around, praying I'd be able to keep my precious cargo safe. Diminutive Willie was wedged into the back seat, and Claude, all six-feet-plus of him, was trying to find comfort on the passenger side. Feeling the inside of the door, his fingers touched one of the many rocks I have tucked inside the car. "Oh, rocks!" he said, smiling. "Yes," I said, laughing. "I have them everywhere. And smooth stones." It seems he collected them as well.

And so our adventure began, with me carefully following his directions and faint-sightedness (the blind leading the blind?) to an experience I'll never forget. Following Claude's lead, we ultimately stopped at a dirt-covered expanse overlooking the north side of the San Diego River Estuary. Claude—who articulates in a high-energy, mercurial style that is dramatic and punctuated with explanation points—explained to us that this was also known as the flood control channel, with its artificially straightened, rock-fortified east-to-west-oriented embankments.

Willie and I took out our little binoculars and attempted to focus in on the various flocks of birds we saw on the distant exposed sand and mud flats. Claude asked us what we saw, and we did our best to describe the various feathered inhabitants that fed and flew and landed there. Claude then thumbed through his weathered bird book and placed the pages as close to his face as possible, still able to grab some visuals, and explained in excited detail what each avian happened to be.

It was as if we were seeing for the first time, soon discovering that each of those birds had a classification, a distinct sound (which Claude easily replicated for us), and markings unique and separate like airborne thumbprints.

Guided by Claude's insightful knowledge, we were now seeing more than a bunch of birds. We were spotting what we learned were brown pelicans, and that large white wader with a yellow bill was a great egret. The smaller, all-dark wader was a little blue heron. Those nondescript, medium-size gray shorebirds were willets, turning into striking black-and-white winged beauties as they took off in flight. The larger brown shorebirds with the long bills feeding on the mudflats were marbled godwits, and resting next to them were western gulls, with white heads and underbellies, dark backs and wings. And that rough, raspy cry we heard belonged to Caspian terns, white birds with black caps and red bills.

It was a plethora of bird sightings. And the incredible thing was that we were witnessing such wonder through the eyes of a nearly sightless man.

At another spot, after I parked the car, Claude pointed out something we would never have noticed in a million years had he not alerted us to it. It was a gigantic osprey nest platform situated high atop a large light assembly for illuminating nighttime sports events in the ball fields there. Noting that many sparrows seemed to be flying into and out of that huge nest, we asked Claude about it. He explained that it was like a bird condo, ideal for hiding in the recesses of such a generous nest. Perfect.

Walking up a narrow hike-and-bike trail, we were nearly run over by an angry bicyclist with an attitude, and then, as we sat on a cement block listening to Claude's ongoing observations, a curious passerby—a lady walking her dog—stopped to ask our wise "professor" some bird questions. Oh, how he loved to answer and offer his lifelong expertise! This was a joy, a passion that fueled him, even as his eyes were now betraying him. But Claude's inner eyesight was so keen, he helped us see and even hear in an entirely new and refreshing way.

For example, right as we departed for our next destination, we noted the rock pigeon nearby. We're so familiar with them everywhere, but did you know that they "clap" their wings once they take off? You can hear them do that if you listen carefully.

And then we heard the different cooing songs of the mourning dove, which sounds more like a "boo-hoo" coo (hence the sorrowful name) as opposed to the gentle lullaby, almost purring, coo of the Eurasian collared dove. Once Claude pointed out the uniqueness of each bird call, the distinction was so clear.

At last we headed back to a sequestered wildlife preserve tucked right inside a residential area, like a secret garden known only to those who seek it out and love it.

I parked in front of a little trail, and we negotiated down into a designated tidally-influenced wetland estuarine. The entire area received salty water from the San Diego River and fresh runoff water from surrounding areas. It was beautiful.

Finding a small bench, we sat and watched and listened to the symphony of nature surrounding us. As we munched on muffins and trail mix, our senses were tuned into a world of sights and sounds Claude helped us experience with delight. Everywhere we looked, there were lovely yellow and white daisies blossoming inside the rocky outcroppings. Claude explained that they were actually called Garland Chrysanthemums, a nonnative annual plant. And those other daisy-like yellow flowers with the dark centers were California encelia. They bloomed all along the leafy bushes outlining the trails.

What was that orangey, low-growing straggly mass spread across many of the bushes? Claude said that was a dodder, a parasitic plant that attaches to low vegetation found along the shoreline. We sat and took it all in, listening to the lovely sounds of the common yellowthroat, the song sparrow, and the house finch singing from the nearby bushy vegetation. Claude helped us hear their different calls.

But it was the northern mockingbird that especially thrilled (trilled?) me. The fact that Claude was a member of the reading group that I led, along with Jeana and David and Lynn (I was reading *To Kill a Mockingbird* to them every week), seemed to be the coup de grâce of this special morning. Not only did we hear the sweet song of the mockingbird, but Claude pointed out that this little bird was so named because it "mocked" the sounds of other birds so perfectly you can't tell that it's a ploy. But Claude knew instantly that it was a mockingbird imitating another bird! I am still blown away by the remarkable ear and keen intelligence of this genius biologist.

There are certain moments, times, days that are highlights. I'm sure you have them too. But this is one of those memories that will always cause me to smile. And to push me to be more aware. And be more grateful. To appreciate every lovely life moment and the gift of my senses taking it into my soul, never to be forgotten. And to know a nearly blind bird man named Claude, who has helped me see and hear the beauty of nature in ways I had never done before. It was so worth the drive. And Claude must have thought so too, because he said he'd do it again. With me behind the wheel. Amazing.

The best and most beautiful things in the world cannot be seen or even touched - they must be felt with the heart.

—HELEN KELLER

LESSON FROM BLIND BIRDING BY THE BAY:

Even if you can't see or walk or tap into any of your other senses, the strength and beauty and power of the natural world awaken the soul to a deeper appreciation—an inner sight. See nature with your heart, and you'll be surprised at what you're able to learn and feel.

People need nature. Nature doesn't need people.

—HARRISON FORD

Man is the most insane species. He worships an invisible God and destroys a visible Nature. Unaware that the Nature he is destroying is this God he is worshipping.

—HUBERT REEVES

CHAPTER 16

THE NAUTILUS

Life is a journey. When we stop, things don't go right.

—POPE FRANCIS

Build thee more stately mansions, O my soul...
Let each new temple, nobler than the last,
Shut thee from heaven with a dome more vast,
Till thou at length art free,
Leaving thine outgrown shell by life's unresting sea!

—OLIVER WENDELL HOLMES

THE BEAUTIFUL CHAMBERED nautilus offers one of the most difficult and yet most important lessons of all: that of the almost impossible act of letting go. I'll explain, but envision now that sea creature's lovely vacated home, usually white with brownish bands on the outside. In scientific terms, the nautilus is known as *Nautilus pompilius,* and it lives in the Indian and Pacific Oceans. This tropical sea creature has numerous slender tentacles around its mouth, with a well-developed head and large eyes. Buoyant with its gas-filled shell upright, allowing it to descend to greater depths during the day, the nautilus migrates vertically at sundown from depths of two thousand feet up to three hundred feet as it seeks its prey. It then returns to the deepest part of the ocean at sunrise.

Considered one of the planet's living fossils, they have remained basically unchanged for millions of years, first appearing about 500 million years ago during the Cambrian explosion. That's 265 million years before dinosaurs inhabited the earth! Talk about survival skills. (If it weren't for humans constant collecting of their beautiful shells and their slow reproduction rate, they might even be more plentiful and not near extinction along with the planet's other endangered species.)

This tropical marine cephalopod is also related to the squid, cuttlefish, and octopus families. But unlike its relatives, the nautilus has something distinct, among other differing features: an external shell. But you don't get to see the intricacy of this extraordinary sea creature's inner life unless it exits and its shell is split open, cut in half, enabling you to see its pearly interior, the lustrous mother-of-pearl nacre, the sinewy stairway of small to large series of chambers, like an inner cornucopia. The shell itself exhibits a unique countershading—light on the bottom and dark on top. The reason? To help avoid predators, because when seen from above, it blends into the darkness of the sea, and when seen from below, it blends in with the light coming from above.

I love the fact that the name nautilus comes from the Greek word for sailor, implying that the shellfish symbolizes a sailor, and that its shell is the ship in which it sails. Everything about it is designed to move and survive and grow.

But here's the thing, and why I am showcasing this lovely sea being at all—not to teach you Chambered Nautilus 101, though everything about its adaptations is fascinating. No, the main reason I'm talking about the nautilus is its ability to keep on developing within its brand-new chamber while shutting the door to the last one. For as the animal grows, its body moves forward with a wall called a septum simply sealing off the older chambers, and as Thomas Wolfe said, it "—can't go home again."

Home is now its new chamber, where its body is completely contained. A leathery hood shuts it in and protects it from predators.

I have grown more drawn to this seaside metaphor as I focus on each new chapter of my life. Like the chambers of the nautilus itself, each of us embodies separate realities that grow forever—forcing us to literally live and stretch and think outside the box. Because, as with the nautilus, each path, each chamber, points the way forward, not backward. Indeed, even if we wanted to occupy the exact place we left behind, we can't. We have changed. Life as we knew it has changed. We no longer fit into that old place. The doors are shut, as they are meant to be.

That's what the nautilus sea creature is all about. Evolving. If it stayed in its present chamber or attempted to go backward, it would die. It has no choice but to grow forward and move on. It must continually build newer, larger additions to its shell.

As Christ told his flock, "In my Father's house, there are many mansions." We all have many mansions within us. But in order to truly live in them, we can't, we mustn't allow ourselves to become trapped within a single chamber that has become too small for us. We are here to grow as we build newer, larger perspectives, until one day we break free of our earthly shells and are, as the great Dr. Martin Luther King Jr. said, "Free at last, free at last. Thank God almighty, we are free at last."

Make your mistakes, take your chances, look
silly, but keep on going. Don't freeze up.

—THOMAS WOLFE

LESSON FROM THE NAUTILUS TEACHER:

The nautilus encourages us to stand back and see life's journeys from this ever-winding, infinite growing of passage to passage as we let go of, reflect upon, and learn from the past and yet continue to grow into the present and future. There are so many dimensions to each of us. And the only way we can truly live our purpose is to continue on the path, experiencing each new awareness in a larger, more global perspective. If we understand that going home to that exact place we once were is no longer an option, we are forced to seek new horizons waiting before us.

Nobody gets to live life backward. Look
ahead, that is where your future lies.

—ANN LANDERS

Just as a snake sheds its skin, we must shed
our past over and over again.

—BUDDHA

CHAPTER 17

THE LOBSTER

Growth means change and change involves risk, stepping
from the known to the unknown.

— GEORGE SHINN

THE LOBSTER ALSO has much to teach us about shedding the discomfort of our present condition in order to grow forward. Literally. Indeed, the only way this large marine crustacean is able to evolve into a larger and more mature aspect of itself is to use the stimulus of stress in order to squeeze out of its present rigid state of being—that is, a shell that has become far too tight. The process happens throughout its lifetime, and it's not easy, either, yet in order to live, it must continually rid itself of what no longer fits. Once its old shell becomes too constrictive, that's when it begins to transform.

It's a struggle to claw out of that confining shell, but the lobster instinctively knows that unless it leaves it behind, it will be stuck in a small space that will ultimately cause it to suffocate and die. Unless it sheds its old layer, the healthier, stronger one beneath cannot expand.

This is the part I find so fascinating: while the lobster is changing clothes from too tight to just right, hiding as best as it can under a rocky place beneath the sea, that's the time when it's most vulnerable to predators. Because during that transition from old to new, that's when it's naked and its new shell hasn't yet formed the protective hard covering around it. And yet it courageously goes through the process of removing itself from its constricting shell—risking its life in order to enable itself to be unencumbered and thrive once again.

LESSON FROM THE LOBSTER TEACHER:

In order to fully transform out of our present condition of discomfort, whether that is a mental or physical state of being—the familiar feeling of being "stuck" in a rigid situation that no longer fits our needs—we need to shed what no longer suits us to be able to breathe, grow, stretch, and thrive. If we don't get out from under what is holding us back, we could even suffocate and die from the stress and pain. Even if the change we inherently desire makes us feel naked in our new vulnerability, the reality is that continuous change is ultimately just what we need to face new perspectives and gather new strength and understanding.

*To exist is to change, to change is to mature, to mature
is to go on creating oneself endlessly.*

—Henri Bergson

*There will come a time when you believe
everything is finished. That will be the beginning.*

—Louis L'Amour

What is life? It is the flash of a firefly in the night. It is the breath of a buffalo in the wintertime. It is the little shadow which runs across the grass and loses itself in the sunset.

—BLACKFOOT

God made the wild animals of the earth of every kind,
and the cattle of every kind,
and everything that creeps upon the ground
of every kind. And God saw that it was good.

GENESIS 1:25

Animals are indeed more ancient, more complex, and in many ways more sophisticated than man. In terms of Nature they are truly more perfect because they remain within the ordered scheme of Nature and live as Nature intended. They are different to us, honed by natural selection over millennia so they should not be patronised, but rather respected and revered. And of all the animals, perhaps the most respected and revered should be the Elephant, for not only is it the largest land mammal on earth, but also the most emotionally human.

—DAME DAPHNE SHELDRICK

MOTHER NATURE IS CALLING YOU

The best remedy for those who are afraid, lonely or
unhappy is to go outside, somewhere where they can be
quiet, alone with the heavens, nature and God. Because
only then does one feel that all is as it should be.

—ANNE FRANK

WHAT IS THE best way to experience the strength that Mother Nature offers? Here are some suggestions for you no matter what your age or stage in life—whether you're single, an aunt, an uncle, a parent, a grandparent, a teacher, or simply a major lover of life!—to get outside and discover the natural environment that awaits. Every. Single. Moment. So temporarily put away all the electronic gadgets we have convinced ourselves that we cannot live without and to the tune of the legendary Crosby, Stills, Nash, and Young song "Teach Your Children," do just that. Teach your children (and your own self, your own inner child!) about life outside your door, and help them become an integral part of living and breathing in the natural world. From placing a tiny bean in a cup in their bedroom and watching it grow to planting seeds together in a little plot outside somewhere, that is how you can begin to share the natural wonders that await. And yes, let them get their hands dirty as they learn to plant bigger gardens that yield fresh and oh so healthy bounty for your meals, and have them shovel and get sweaty and feel the morning sun on their backs and then stargaze at night, counting the constellations. And when it begins to pour, grab their boots and slickers and dance in the rain. I did that with my boys when they were little, and those are some of my most favorite memories of us together. Sloshing in mud puddles and following creeks and exploring caves just blocks from where we lived. That was far better than any paid amusement park. And you didn't have to stand in line to leapfrog a puddle, either! Or, indeed, to appreciate the delight of a frog or cricket chorus when you stopped talking and simply listened. Mother Nature is a constant event. You can't put a price tag on the fascination of watching a stream of ants working tirelessly, carrying their food and eggs in and out of such ingenious tunnels and mounds. Or seeking out a camouflaged lizard or bird or tortoise or bug and wondering how amazingly each is so protected from its prey with many adaptations for hiding in plain sight. Hanging out with Mother Nature instantly transforms us into both teacher and student. The learning and discovering never stop.

Whether you like to walk, jog, hike, mountain climb, or whale watch, go birding or tide pooling, camp out or go whitewater rafting or surf, garden, take up wildlife photography or drawing, kayak or canoe, snorkel, scuba dive, or just hug a tree or three on a daily basis—opportunities abound to appreciate the natural wonders everywhere. From dog walking to helping animal rescue sanctuaries, the choices are infinite, just like your hopeful choice to support industries that practice animal conservation rather than those corporate greed-based organizations that promote capturing and exploiting animals in the name of entertainment.

There are unbounded variables—so many ways to both help and appreciate Mama Nature. Must-reads include anything the brilliant naturalist, author, and scriptwriter Sy Montgomery has written, including what have become my bibles, *The Soul of an Octopus* and *The Good, Good Pig: The Extraordinary Life of Christopher Hogwood*. I love these books so much I really cried when I finished them. And then, of course, I had to read them again. If I could have a pet octopus and a pet pig right now, I would be the happiest lady on the planet. And it's all Sy's fault! As so aptly described in *The Boston Globe*, Sy Montgomery is "part Indiana Jones and part Emily Dickinson." She has written well over twenty books on just about every species. Her writing is so engaging and beautiful that you find yourself falling in love with everything, from tarantulas to sea snakes, to everything that flies, crawls, and pounces, just because she has that magical ability to teach as well as entertain with great compassion! I give her books as gifts to those who love animals as much as I do.

Then, you really must check out Dr. Jane Goodall's global program, "Roots & Shoots" (www.rootsandshoots.org/), which involves young people from preschool to university age to work on environmental, conservation, and humanitarian issues. And it's even fun to do! Another must-see website is the Children & Nature Network (www.childrenandnature. org/), which connects you to worldwide leaders, each helping to unite and build an important synergy between children and nature. Or why not carve out a niche where your passion to protect wildlife is also your actual job, such as Animal Legal Defense Fund lawyers, who work on animal protection? There is a multitude of tree-planting organizations you could join, like Tree People (www.treepeople.org). One Tree Planted (www.one-treeplanted.org) plants trees all over the world. If you have a particular skill, don't be afraid to use it to donate pro bono work to worthy causes. The National Anti-Vivisection Society is dedicated to ending the exploitation of animals used in science. Or think of becoming a doctor and using your skills to continue advancements in science that don't involve animal testing (and definitely boycott all products that do test on animals!) or volunteer with Doctors Without Borders (www.doctorswithoutborders.org) or one of the many other extraordinary organizations like it that are helping to fulfill a global need for medical care. I won't go into the infinite ways you can begin to protect and preserve this blessed planet—including not eating meat and definitely planting trees, which save the world in probably the most powerful ways of all. Just start doing your research.

There are myriad websites, books, documentaries, experts, and more helping us learn about what we can and must do to help save our precious planet. Go online, listen to TED talks and podcasts, and read and embrace what knowledgeable earth advocates are teaching. Just one baby step taken each day creates a positive ripple effect. Everything helps!

Praised be You, my Lord, through Sister Earth
our Mother, who sustains and governs us.

—St. Francis of Assisi

EPILOGUE

*Very little grows on jagged rock. Be ground. Be
crumbled. So wildflowers will come up—where you
are. You have been stony for too many years.
Try something different. Surrender*

—RUMI

THE THING IS this: no matter what you're going through in your life,
you always have the opportunity to find a sense of peace and perspective within nature. There is a lesson as well as a teacher in everything.
The few teachers I've discussed here in this book are multiplied tenfold
everywhere you look, all over the world.

I would have to create a book the size of the entire world to en-
compass all the Nature Teachers on our planet. Every single day I learn
something new about the multitude of the voiceless being slaughtered,
captured, enslaved, made to perform, considered as nothing but food or
fashion accessories, rather than the soulful, intelligent, vibrant, exquisite, compassionate, forgiving, joyful beings they happen to be. Forests
across the world are being torn down and dismantled for everything
from palm oil to parking lots. Nature Teachers are everywhere, offering
us purity and a living, breathing life force that we humans are choking
off into nonexistence. So much like Shel Silverstein's beautiful book *The
Giving Tree*. Nature doesn't stop giving to us, this selfish, narcissistic human species determined to destroy it. (I'm so grateful to know some

mighty advocates, including animal activist, Ellen Ericksen, who are so courageously fighting for the voice of this precious planet to be heard and honored. There are far too many to list here, but I've never known braver or more passionate warriors.)

The handful of teachers I speak about in this book are but symbols, representing millions of other species with voices and stories that need to be told and heard and protected as well. Just as Anne Frank has become a messenger for the oppressed and destroyed in continuous human and nonhuman holocausts, each of the beings in this book represents all of them—from elephants to orcas to ants, amphibians, reptiles, octopuses, fish, apes, dogs, cats, birds, bears, bees, every exotic and farm-raised animal and insect, flowers, blades of grass, trees, plants, weeds, and on and on—that are alive today. We must never forget their place in our world as essential links to every single one of us. Some wonderful day, I pray with all my heart, we will honor them as we honor ourselves and realize that all species are all *one* and must be cherished and protected forever equally.

Nature Teachers abound on the land and in the sea, in the air, and deep within the earth. When you take the time to savor the moment, to sit with what is happening before you and let yourself truly experience it, then the light goes on. What is outside is within. And what is within is outside. Everything in the natural world is a reflection of your own self. All you have to do is watch and listen and breathe and feel and touch what is surrounding you. Then ask yourself, "What can I learn from this? Where can I find the strength in this?" You'll be surprised at how quickly an answer appears.

Whatever it is you're challenged with right now, I promise you there is a Nature Teacher waiting to reflect back to you a message of hope, peace, patience, humor, and acceptance to help you. Look around. Nature Teachers are everywhere. The tiniest weed poking through a crack in the sidewalk. An ant lugging a crumb three times its size. Trees and bushes gracefully outstretched and surprisingly thriving within the confines of a crowded parking lot or the asphalt jungle of a freeway embankment. Indeed, in the most unlikely places we'd never think to look, just around the corner from most of us, there are small trails and protected preserves filled with tall grasses, wildflowers, bees, butterflies, and rain-soaked ponds harboring egrets, herons, pheasants, ducks, geese, bullfrogs, quail, hawks, hares, lizards, snakes, birds of all species, and a multitude of insects—all within confined areas bordered by condos, houses, office buildings, shopping centers, and parking lots. Just outside the city limits, even deer, coyotes and bobcats survive.

In spite of human encroachment the strength of nature prevails against all odds.

Even the brutal, horrific aftermath of a natural disaster ultimately gives way to new life—like the singular pine tree that withstood the 2011 tsunami in Japan. It remained a sign of hope for all—as did the cherry blossoms, becoming a symbol of survival even after what appeared to be the end of all life. (There is a must-see award-winning documentary called *The Tsunami and the Cherry Blossom* by director Lucy Walker and producers Kira Carstensen and Aki Mizutani.)

And, of course, there is the Survivor Tree, the legendary nearly hundred-year-old American elm at the Oklahoma City National Memorial and Museum (www.oklahomacitynationalmemorial.org). Having lived through a horrific bomb blast, the Survivor Tree has now become a symbol of survival from one of the worst terrorist attacks on American soil. Cuttings and seeds from this mighty bastion of resilience are now growing into thousands of Survivor Trees all over the United States!

This is also true for the large horse chestnut tree that Anne Frank looked out upon while she was in hiding. The graceful tree seemed to buoy her hopes and dreams for a better future, symbolizing freedom as well as the beauty of nature, which she longed to enjoy once again. Thankfully, the stewards at the Anne Frank House created saplings from the aging tree as it collapsed from disease in 2010. Today, these saplings, which originated in Amsterdam, are distributed all across the United States thriving at schools and memorial centers (http://annefrank.com/the-sapling-project). Anne's legacy of hope lives on.

The strength we can gather from nature is mighty. Think of the indomitable and eternally beautiful Monterey pine and others in the pine family, which actually reproduce and grow stronger after forest fires. How can that be? Mother Nature doesn't throw in the towel, even when leveled time and time again.

Nature is everywhere we are. In the stifling confines of a windowless room there is a moth, a fly, a spider, some busy bug strolling across the floor, up a wall, or down a potted plant—some hint of nature to help guide us back to our own inner realities. Take time and really see it. We're never separate from the natural world. We're all linked together as earthly beings in this Earth School.

We, as humans, are no different from the other students and teachers in our lives—all of us, human and nonhuman. All are reflections of one another in some way. Our coverings and lifestyles may be unique, but in infinite ways we're the same. For me, this is a realization that provides great comfort. I like knowing that I'm never alone in my quest to find balance in this human form I'm rattling around in. It's seeing or feeling ourselves separate from one another that feeds into feelings of alienation and disquietude. In truth, we're all connected.

So take this little book as a guide to help you see your own reflection in life. How are you like that patch of weeds, field of wheat, stalking cat, running dog, rainbow, rain cloud, parking lot tree, or ladybug? What is the natural world doing to simply *be* what it is, to survive against all odds, to live every single moment with grace and acceptance—and to help you accept who you are as well? The answers are always there. There are pieces of us in everything.

In this book I've focused on just a few Nature Teachers that have helped me. As I have expressed, there are other Nature Teachers just like them wherever you go. Watch them. Listen to them. See how they deal with and accept the challenges they experience—from ravaging fires to leveling hurricanes, tornadoes, and epic floods. The answers are as simple as the questions. And the beauty is that if we let them, they'll help us cope with the most challenging task of all: being human. I wish you the blessings of discovery on your path. And ultimately the love of life—within and surrounding you. There is innate strength and power and light to be found in the natural world—and deep within all that *you* are. This strength and power and light are everywhere you look and breathe and touch and feel. Nature simply *is*. Just like you.

ABOUT THE AUTHOR

Photo Credit:
Lauren Lang
Jacobin Photography

CARA WILSON-GRANAT IS dedicated to learning about and defending Mother Nature as an author, devoted animal activist, vegan, and inspirational speaker. She is also the author of *Strength from Tragedy: Anne Frank's Father Shares His Wisdom with an American Teen*. Otto Frank's compassionate insight has guided Wilson-Granat through many challenges in her life, especially helping her believe in the power of hope through one planted tree at a time. Cara lives with her husband, Peter, and cat, Boo, in Colorado.

ABOUT THE ILLUSTRATOR

Photo Credit:
Steffani Liskey Photography

EMILY TAIT IS a pediatric nurse by night, mixed media painter and mountain-climbing adventurer by day. She loves nothing more than to share love and compassion with people through her nursing career and her paintings. Emily lives in Denver, Colorado for now and will be moving to Uganda to pursue her dream of serving as a missionary nurse.

88635447R00057

Made in the USA
Columbia, SC
01 February 2018